THROUGH
MY EYES

THROUGH MY EYES

Vicky McCarthy Keane

Through My Eyes
Published in 2021 by Vicky McCarthy Keane

Copyright © Vicky McCarthy Keane

ISBN: 978-1-7399249-0-4

All rights reserved. No part of this publication may be reproduced or transmitted in any form or by any means, electronic or mechanical, including photography, recording, or any information storage or retrieval system without permission in writing from Vicky McCarthy Keane. The book is sold subject to the condition that it shall not, by way of trade or otherwise, be lent, copied, altered, resold or otherwise circulated without Vicky McCarthy Keane's prior consent in any form of binding or cover other than that in which is published and without similar a condition, including this condition, being imposed on any subsequent publisher.

Editing & publishing consultancy provided by Jeremy Murphy of JM Editing & Literary Agency
www.jermurphy.com

I dedicate this book to my husband Michael and our four children Stephen, Lauren, Lucas and Rachel. They each gave me the strength and encouragement that I needed to complete this, my first book. Endless love to them always and forever.

Contents

Burren Winter Before I Sleep 1

Kreuth Forest in Deep Winter 3

Red Robin and I. 5

The Weeping Willow 7

The Twisted Path 8

Moon Secrets 10

A Wild Wind 12

Lost. 13

The Day it Rained All Day 14

Farewell Anjouan 16

The Lost Years 18

Griston Bog 19

My Tree of Hope 20

Window of Words 21

The Flaggy Shore	23
The Whispering Pines	25
Elysian Memories	26
Peace	28
Sunset over Fanore	29
About the Author	31

Burren Winter Before I Sleep

I hear you call through an angry windswept shore,
your beauty grey but gently so,
too soon to follow your beckoning whisper,
as howling winds hide your cruel intention.

Be patient my friend with your dismal thoughts,
for there are memories yet to lay before you,
through hazel woodland you search for me,
disturbing pygmy shrews and pine martens in your flurry.

You follow me under a sleepy moon,
your presence cutting through the cry of a lonesome curlew.
I hear your footsteps closer now,
sweet scent of earthy clay under cladded fingertips.

Through hazel shrub,widgeons and golden plovers hide,
guided by the beacon of a distant lighthouse.
Wood mice scurry through damp walls and crevices,
feeding on black ivy berries with oblivious gaze.

Through My Eyes

Through misted panes four sombre faces stare,
their loneliness shadowed by the dark night,
guided by a new life of hopes and dreams,
and the promise of further togetherness.

Be still my friend for I must follow you now,
shroud me in your eternal grip,
for I have loved and been loved,
and wander beside you peacefully to the end.

Kreuth Forest in Deep Winter

The sleigh horses clip clopped into a soft canter,
as heavy skies hung dark grey on grey.
You followed as we crunched and bumped,
through the muffled mouth of Kreuth Forest.

It was surely bitter now, but laden in beauty.
Powdered pines waved as we cowered past,
bowing graciously as snow slid and fell gently
into our path, that you knew oh so well.

Pebbled and covered in yellowed white,
we raced and panted along tracks of old.
I felt you closer as you whistled and whimpered,
only pausing to catch your laboured breath.

As you bravely blew past shaking our grip,
the horse petal bells jingled loud and crisp.
I could not see you, and with but a muted mouth
silenced by your cruel hand, there could be no retort.

Through My Eyes

Snow flakes drifted sideways through a misted blur,
as we tucked and tugged on our dampened horse blanket.
Pillared pines swayed softly and grew thin on thin,
as a lifted mist unveiled three paths of old.

The coachman with the feathered hat did not pause,
to ponder on the past and the future.
As you whooshed briskly past one last time,
we took the path marked "present", and bid you farewell.

Red Robin and I

Two years, six months, four days,
you perch with grace upon my sill,
blackened soil upon clasped talons,
rousing feathers on a bitter crisp morn.

With a whisper song you beckon me closer,
with every chirp comes familiar prattle,
a heart brimmed with endearment,
a life vivacious to its painful end.

Across a crimson sky we drift,
over distant dreams and aged memories.
You tell me to never look back,
as many bridges we do cautiously cross.

We turn towards your forever place,
drifting in and out of tree tops and thoughts.
Alas, a cross stands proudly in the night sky,
hovering over fields of stone and clotted clay.

Through My Eyes

Through golden gates you lay me down,
as you turn to me and stare,
fear not my beloved friend,
rest now as we turn to bid farewell.

The Weeping Willow

Oh my lonesome one, deep rooted in thought,
you bury flowing locks in clasped branches,
heaving heavily neath the garden brook,
as the dew drops plink from your tender tresses.

Medusa was once a mortal beauty
who suffered at the hands of Athena,
she too like you was cursed, her precious locks
morphed into a hideous head of snakes.

You are placed there by the lily pond,
where a robin pecks and hops amongst the clay,
such a peaceful place for you to lay your roots,
for the friends of old to ponder in splendour.

Hebe will grant you eternal youth,
an immortality worthy of a deity of the soul,
never wilting as the seasons wander by,
your beauty never fading in the minds of the many.

The Twisted Path

I stand before you with a brave smile,but
who are you that shook the cones from the branch,
that choked the sodden trees with blackened ivy,
and pulled the dewy cobwebs from the bush.

I followed you up a long twisted path,
in search of a portal to some heavenly land,
from the dizzy merry dances of blue bearded irises,
to the gentle swish sway of dandelion seeds.

Many listened to wild weary whisperings
of poisoned pines of the forest,
never to feel a warm breeze over wrinkled brow,
or taste sweet droplets of joy from a giddy birch.

Many hills did I climb to reach you,
stumbling over bundles of hope and angered gorse,
panting, searching, looking back with fear,
alas peace from the darkness left behind.

Vicky McCarthy Keane

You reach out through a sleepy moon,
gently kneeling under twinkling stars of hope,
haunted humming from a nearby hungered field,
draws you close as I breathe softly now.

Moon Secrets

Silver twinklings over a blotted bay,
a muted misted moon finds its way,
through smokey clouds of yellowed grey,
hiding peeping alas shining proudly.

Oh moody moon over giddy waters,
you cast a dark light over rotten ridges,
you shed heavy teardrops of bitter farewells,
oh why did you hide from the needy.

Night shadows crawl over dewy fields of old,
carrying silenced secrets of a hungered land.
A moonlit cottiers cottage battered broken,
once brimmed with soft song and proud prattle.

A folding tide spits out softened spray,
as the shrill mew call of circling seagulls,
falls over land of once blackened leaf,
echoing the shrieking cry of pained paupers.

Vicky McCarthy Keane

You danced the dance of love and hope
as you watched the weary fall to their knees,
lost souls buried with unmarked dreams,
oh why did you hide from the needy.

A Wild Wind

A wild wind did howl my way,
creaking croaking never caring,
oh who sent you into my path
to pluck the petals from the rose.

Hold back distant dreary one,
no chase can halt your sprightly step,
twixt brambles and briars you do wander,
sweeping up memories of a treasured past.

With a wink of a widgeon's stare
you ramble over glen and glory,
never one to chitter chatter,
no blue bearded irises lay in your path.

With panting breath upon my back
you dance neath the gap of a feidín wall,
one final step you pull me close
and lead me to where the listless lilies lie.

Lost

In bleak mid-winter day became night,
serenity of silence was no more,
incessant tapping on my pane,
tempestuous night like no other.

Fear not my gentle soul,
we will ride the waves together,
turbulent waters rise high,
and hold you in their angry grip.

Muttering hum of prayers from below,
footsteps nervously pacing under foot,
alas that feared gentle knock,
creaking floor holds its breath.

Verbose and softly spoken
in unison with the whistle of the wind,
a mother wails on her knees,
a child, a brother, lost forever.

The Day it Rained All Day

Curtains drawn tight on a black morn,
utterings of a dreaded kind,
a heart frozen with fear,
oh how it poured that day.

Muffled murmurs from afar,
oh how it passed over my head,
a white coat she did wear that day,
she wasn't the one to get wet.

She held my hand limp and cold,
it was surely pouring now,
she did not say the rain would stop,
but there would be sun some days.

Oh how it still pours some days,
even on a warm sunny day,
the image of four little faces,
the words of an old love song.

Sweet memories of those early years,
when life flew past without a care,
oh grab the love and hold it tight,
for tomorrow it may pour all day.

Farewell Anjouan

Oh rivers of Anjouan wild and free,
once brimmed with life never lost in dreams,
cascading over free flowing falls,
yellowed fluttered beauty flapping with life.

Who stole the birds from the trees
or felt the flow of tears be but a trickle,
who felled the giant trees of hope,
choking the breath from the mouths of the needy.

Once loud and roaring with wondrous joy,
twisting and turning neath a burning sun,
now bereft of life's pleasures and past,
silenced by some cruel hunter of the lost.

Oh Anjouan for you are like me,
battered broken numb to the touch,
empty of any semblance of normality,
fighting for the strength to be free.

Vicky McCarthy Keane

Farewell Anjouan my friend,
for unlike me you can be free again
to watch the rivers run wild
and sow the seeds of future dreams.

The Lost Years

Rotten ridges over blackened clay,
deathly stench of pitied paupers,
oh who stole the lives of the languished,
and banished the broken to distant shores.

Oh famine queen of wealth and glory,
no broth did pass your lavish lips,
reliefs to tease the flesh from the bone,
oh dear god how they turned on their own.

Barrows stacked with forgotten mortals,
unturned sod over a blighted land,
no cross to etch loss upon loss,
no dignity for a parting soul.

To Russell we did relinquish our gain,
with his high buckled boots capped in clay,
evictions to the gangways for weary cottiers,
oh dear god how they turned on their own.

Griston Bog

One half perch had we to bluster,
an ass and cart we knew no wonder,
rusty aged slean knew many a tale,
fond memories for many to ponder.

Bewitching earthy smell of moss underfoot,
purple moor grass under a burning sun,
backbreaking sigh of a barrowman,
bootless pale turf every catcher did shun.

Sparrow sandmartin and swallow,
lurking lordly in shrouded ditches,
waterflies lingering over deathly bogholes,
a lone kingfisher crowned in midges.

Sullied kettle laden in spring water,
sodden brown sandwiches, buttermilk and tea,
bog briars and crooked brambles we did reach,
tannin on barefeet as weary as could be.

My Tree of Hope

I dreamt I had a tree of hope
on a high heavenly hill,
it danced with a wild westerly wind,
sweeping swaying swirling.

With spinning apples so shiny and sweet,
like sugar coated happy hearts,
oh no rotten blackened fruit
did fall my merry way.

With ancient twisted briars
and open armed branches,
it hugged the longing and the lonely,
where touch is free without a care.

With the gentle whistle of a warm wind,
it whispered promises of togetherness,
for all who dream of a tree of hope,
will taste the fruit of happiness.

Window of Words

I sit there by the window,
hunched over and lost in a world
of fluttering dreams, whose mood
flips with the seasons beyond.

Today you are grey no more
as you fuel my mind aplenty.
A steady breeze blows the rhythm
of thought and reason over and back.

I believe you sense when I am here,
drinking you in with every glance,
your gentle folding and lapping,
sweet music to my pensive journey.

A soft shower taps gently on an
oily pane of multi prism beauty.
The blotted ink trickles and dribbles
making sense of it all as if by plan.

Yesterday you roared and spat out
swirls of frothy spray with sheer anger,
a freak bolt turning grey to darkest black,
you knew the words were but a dream.

A wild wind howled and shook the thatch,
whistling up and down the flue,
billowing earthy scent of turf
in choking circles of blackened soot.

You blew over on the far side of midnight,
leaving me drowsy on bitter scented candle wax,
floating in and out of thoughts,
as words do not follow on poetic fervour alone.

The Flaggy Shore

Oh rolling hills of mossy grey,
how you fold gently to the raging shore,
a land bewitched with aged fairy forts,
brimmed with giddy dances of an ancient past.

Gentle spray over whittled brow,
slippery crunch underfoot,
the cheeky stare of a feral goat,
pensive, poised, never pitied.

Oh thicket of red winterberry holly,
no folly to a wise old pine marten,
incessant ding of parochial tune
joins the chorus of a hopeful hymn.

Ke Ke Ke neath a setting sun,
a sparrowhawk hops betwixt hazel shrubs,
it's hopeful call resounds through rugged woodland,
in songs of praise for those lost, never forgotten.

Across a foggy distant glen
dogs bark in unison to welcome the night sky,
smokey clouds creep over a crimson display,
promise of a new dawn turning light into hope.

The Whispering Pines

Deep in a damp dense forest
standing tall and oh so proud,
are the ancient but wise whispering pines,
who bow gently to a westerly wind.

Swish sway, swish sway, swish sway,
what sweet music to those who dare
to trust the paths of no return
and brave the dance of happiness.

You blow the leaves of copper and gold,
in swirling circles of hope and love,
oh those who sit on your seat for two,
will feel the warm breeze on their back.

For I did wander your winding way,
to follow your whisperings of old,
and you did point to a silver hill,
alas never did I need to return.

Elysian Memories

Seaweed breeze drifts with excitement
through a car fuelled on giddiness.
A burnt orange sun melts down on
the boisterous curiosity of youth.

Oh ten pence for the first peek at
the wild wondrous blue on grey,
spitting and sloshing over our
chunk eaten dunes of tufted green.

Barefoot, battling with buckets, brimmed
with innocence, never tainted but by
an incoming tide that swallowed whole shells
and buried blackened rocks neath fizzy foam.

Silted sand drifts stung sharp and deep.
The clod who forgot the windbreaker was
busy knifing a jagged jellyfish, while
yelping and mewing with the circling gulls.

Dizzy from the wild roar lapping and folding,
like a perpetual rapturous applause,
I would stand and face the immortal beast,
alas such Elysian memories as the world bellowed by.

Peace

Gentle breath upon my brow,
such sweet fitful mutterings,
a clasp to rouse warm memories,
your sadness knows no bounds.

A friend a lover and a listener,
a life indebted to your fortitude,
fear superseded by solace,
a gratitude like no other.

Thoughts of everlasting peace,
promises of future affinity,
burning tears over weary face,
forlorn foreboding alas flagging.

Come closer one last time,
with fading breath each listless sigh,
blessings of a peaceful kind,
one final gasp follows fading light.

Sunset over Fanore

Oh here I stand lapping in wondrous peace,
at the yellowed aqua beauty you bequest me,
your blades of green swaddled in porous grey,
not a moment too coveted for a dripping heart.

Come stand beside me my friend of all that is you,
feel the biting brittle breeze cleanse my being,
and let the haunting roar of the great blue yonder,
lay a mantel over a borrowed heart of guarded gold.

As a gull fights against a gallant gale,
you chime the bells of hope from your tower of love.
Where the beacon of old once guided many a mast,
they now take their place as many did before them.

And here we stand with hands tightly clasped,
feet gently blackened in sodden aged clay,
you sing a sweet lullaby with a chorus tainted,
by the saddened mutterings of the chosen ones.

As your orange beauty sinks neath the wild waves,
a silver twinkling path leads me to that place,
where petals never shed from the wild rose,
and tears never fall from your tower of love.

About the Author

Vicky McCarthy Keane is a solicitor, wife to husband Michael and mother to their four children. From an early age she had a great interest in art, in particular pencil sketching and calligraphy. On the 6 November 2017, having recently completed her masters in UCD (LLM), Vicky was diagnosed with motor neuron disease. Never one to say no to a challenge, during the Covid 19 pandemic she took up writing poetry. The inspiration evolved from watching a television programme in which Billy Keane was describing the recent discovery of a copybook belonging to his late father which contains new written work. Since that day Vicky enjoys writing poetry on a daily basis with the assistance of an eye gaze computer.

www.ingramcontent.com/pod-product-compliance
Lightning Source LLC
Chambersburg PA
CBHW020915080526
44589CB00011B/613